UNDER THE RESERVOIR

POETRY
The Collector and Other Poems
The Nature of Cold Weather and Other Poems
At the White Monument and Other Poems
The Force and Other Poems
Work in Progress
Dr Faust's Sea-Spiral Spirit and Other Poems
Three Pieces for Voices
The Hermaphrodite Album (with Penelope Shuttle)
Sons of My Skin: Selected Poems 1954–74
From Every Chink of the Ark
The Weddings at Nether Powers
The Apple-Broadcast and Other New Poems
The Working of Water
The Man Named East and Other New Poems
The Mudlark Poems & Grand Buveur
The Moon Disposes: Poems 1954–1987
In the Hall of the Saurians
The First Earthquake

FICTION
In the Country of the Skin
The Terrors of Dr Treviles (with Penelope Shuttle)
The Glass Cottage
The God of Glass
The Sleep of the Great Hypnotist
The Beekeepers
The Facilitators, or, Madam Hole-in-the-Day
The One Who Set Out to Study Fear

PLAYBOOKS
Miss Carstairs Dressed for Blooding and Other Plays
In the Country of the Skin

PSYCHOLOGY AND WOMEN'S SPIRITUALITY
The Wise Wound (with Penelope Shuttle)
The Black Goddess and the Sixth Sense

UNDER THE RESERVOIR

PETER REDGROVE

Secker & Warburg
POETRY

First published in Great Britain 1992 by
Martin Secker & Warburg Limited
Michelin House, 81 Fulham Road,
London SW3 6RB

A CIP catalogue record for this book
is available from the British Library

ISBN   0 436 41005 2

Printed in Great Britain by
St. Edmundsbury Press, Bury St. Edmunds

CONTENTS

ACKNOWLEDGEMENTS

Acknowledgements are due to the following:

Ambit, *The Manhattan Review*, *Poetry Book Society Supplements 1989* and *1991*, *Poetry Review*, *Poetry USA*, *Times Literary Supplement*

CRY TO THE FISH

He plays sea-shanties on a tin violin,
It has an excellent tone
Under the torch or flambeau
Of fish oil set to light up the
Pilchard gaffer's sails like cinema screens.

The old ship creaked in tune, there was a ghostly
Beer-smell, and as I came in his eyes quibbled
With terror, yet he kept on playing

His shanty to the sea,
And to the fish who that day came swarming to our nets.

The instrument had a fur-lined case
As the cold of the north seas might crystallise it
Into a white and tuneless powder, the power lost
Of tin to cry when made into a violin,
To wail to the fish and all creatures of the deep.

THE SMALL EARTHQUAKE

The birds can't soar because all the breath
That carries them has been withdrawn
Into this great hush, the sea and sky

Calm as two mirrors endlessly reflecting.
Then the stars flicker like candles where a door
Is opened, and closed, and the ground

Bumps slowly, like a ferry as it is steered
Into the quay, bumps on its rope fenders;
And afterwards you cannot believe

The ground shifted; except, high up in the corner
Near the ceiling the white has cracked like a web
Until you try to smear it away: the spider

Under the earth spun it and threw it
Into the house; and I recollect a certain
Tang passed through the air, like

A champagne elixir passing from the abyss, creating
A freshet that soaked the grass, a web-crack,
And a jammed window in Zoe's room upstairs.

THE SECRET EXAMINATION

The wooden desks, the wooden stools
Inscribed with their flow. The examinees

Inscribe their flow. The invigilator
Has a special smell, kindly snapper;

The examinees smell of a good wash
And clean ironing with no black marks;

There is a lean smell of cream and treacle,
Or, as the Bible says, of milk and honey,

For the examination is going well
And distilling by its queries passionless thought

In small puffs from the alembics
Of sleeves and collars

With the tiny writing motions
And slight nods of head; everybody

In this well-lighted room
Of sharp pencils and dazzling pages

And cleanest clothes is exhaling subtexts,
Is inhaling information secretly colluding;

The invigilator knows there is no copying –
But how can all the answers be identical?

He is suspicious of the brightest boy
And the dullest, equally.

BLACKTHORN WINTER

A blackthorn winter. The trees lighter
Than at other times, showing
The inwards of their leaves; the stars
Because of the bitter wind
Twinkle fiercely; the masses of air
Create a hollow echoing in the woodland;
Sunset's slant light rebuilds ghost villages, echoing
In their shadow-plane out of moist deep foundations,
And celtic boundaries pulse in ceaseless wind-markings;

To smell the touch of the wind, to hear the contours.

PINEAL HOUSE

The van drives away, the Christmas Tree
Leans in the front porch, it has
Thousands of green needles; lifted, it is active
And lively with them, like a shark
Which is also a shrub; it takes
Three of us to steer it to its station
In the front room where I unwrap the roots
And we lower them into the broad iron pot.
Jim tamps the rich earth, I fill the watering-can
And wet it with the rose; at once
A full rich smell of pine fills the house,
Like summer mountains taking residence;
Pine-smelling breezes fill the rooms
Like wings beating gently from that tree
While Alice fetches boxes of the amazing
Globes that are mirrors with an entrance
In which a small fat Santa stands and
Six-fingered snowflakes big as your thumb
With hubs of looking glass; there are
A silver dragon and a golden horse, glass apples
Where light lenses at the core, globes
Where it snows on snowmen, and lights
Like tin roses till I plug them in, now they glow
In their tree like a village seen from a plane, like an aurora
Striding through a pine-plantation. We hold the chair
While Alice stretches up to put on the tree's peak
A white-gowned fairy patron princess
Holding a silver staff that breaks into a star;
Now the whole tree is like her green gown
Its folds full of glass residences, budding light,
Fabled beasts riding on their boughs; so then
Arms full we bring them in and pile them up
Against her iron roots, the gifts
Which are further sorceries, and secrets for now.

5

UNDER THE RESERVOIR

The reservoir great as the weight
Of a black sun radiates through the cracks
In the concrete, expresses water supercharged

By pressure and darkness, the whole body
Of water leaning on the hairline cracks,
Water pumping itself through masonry

Like light through glass. Water charged
By the mystery of lying there in storeys
In transparent tons staring both upwards and downwards

(His coffee hand spills on his shirt the regalia
Of his worried mind in linked splashes like medals
Of a muddy war)

The reservoirs in their unending battle to flow
Turned into steely strain like hammered pewter
Endure their thousand tons of mud, as though

They held their surfaces open like Samson
To the dust that sifts on to their cold pewter,
And rejoice in their dark linings, as they might

Rejoice in plentiful seed,
Black seed of illimitable forest cracking
Open the stone rooms when the water has gone.

CARCASS AND BALSAM

The flies drunk on woodland balsams,
And the flies drunk on gross carcasses,
Winged drops of liquid black putrescence,
And winged tears of almost-glass gum:

They display themselves in variety on the window-glass.

The flies like winged coal, burning with hunger;
Magnify their call and it is full of starving voice,
Magnify its muscle and you are in earthquake city
And this is a winged tremor devouring the strata;

And others, almost transparent with manifest tiny guts
Of quartz-clock precision, magnify them and you have
Flying Christmas-trees dangling with bonbons.

As I am in love
I fear and rejoice in the flies equally,
Who like the clouds in flight declare the interactions of all,
And which are flying water perfumed with herbs and shit;

The soul of a man in love
Is full of perfumes and evil smells;
I fear the Evil Odour more than I fear the Evil Eye;

I know from the fly truffling for my sweat
That all of us are both balsam and carcass.

THE BATHSHEBA POEMS

I

If thou forsakest the world
Then thou comest into that
Out of which the world is made.

That glassy rummaging in the dark, that
Darkly-bright place. It tasted
Glossy on my fingers. Little

Footsteps running all over the spine,
A sable zephyr. You've got some size
On you, my man, she remarked.

Her grasp was warm and open, like a hand
Firmly shaken in genuine fellowship; my
Comfort level was now very high,

Her skin the ever-darkening shade
Of wild honey, and I could name the flowers:
Shimmering clover and toxic ivy and

Myrtle that blooms and fruits at once
And is the recourse of trembling bees
All the year round. Moths out of the Cornish night

Arrange themselves on the windscreen in lace pictures.

II

He wore a gold ring
With a moody-looking stone in it.
He sat on the porch, moping in wicker.

His lamp magnetised moths, the landscape
Of his face was illuminated repeatedly
By bolts and twitches of dream-lightning.

He was nursing in the tent of a swollen grudge, in
The dream of it there was a pinhead on which
A man sat fishing.

In youth he was a keen iceman, one who skates
Working his splits and backsprings with the hiss
Of ripping silk; that was until sex

Converted his skills, he was
A very balanced undresser, you hardly noticed
Your things were off except for the hiss

Of silks like snakes of Isis; thus her
Dusky stockings were a self-bewitching memory.
Where could these two go, that was private?

Grey paint was peeling
Off the huffing boiler
In scrolls like scripture, a dinky

Young man with a cast in one eye led them
Down a flight of iron steps under
Shielded bulbs; the cellar had been made

Prettier than the house, and smelt better.
He was still the tummyless athlete, on that occasion
Bathsheba dried herself thirteen times.

9

III

There is a little porthole into the atrium.
Inside, a snake flutters with a winkless eye,
Is it a dysangel? His strong body

Attracts women as the sky the bird. The sun
Kindled eternal fire in the sapphire
Of the ocean, spread out like Lucifer's throne

Pulsing and transforming with the dark angel's moods.
And Bathsheba went in unto the King
In his chamber, and Rabbi Judah said 'On that occasion

Bathsheba dried herself thirteen times.' After that
There were as many solemn chimes on the bell
To signify a Goddess was present. Lucifer's throne

Darkened through the window, but then
Thunderstorms came wheeling in, rainwater
Cascaded through caves and tunnels making noises

Like flocks of birds throughout
The rackety town of off-white buildings like
Enormous birdshit dropped on the granite hills.

After Bathsheba's triumph everything,
Not just the sea, was full of angels, the daffodils in the
  bathroom
Vase shone like Stars of David, as did the good-

Humoured pug nose of the hot-water tap that bestowed on
  them
Their bath together. Now he would have his house
Built of Dorset brick fetched here to please

His Dorset-born Bathsheba, having seen the sea
Simultaneously changing as he took his woman, and come
To a certain conclusion.

NOMADS

The fields, the meadows of grass
In the clear space, the moor
Over the town, high up, among the
Aerial seeds. There are no buildings
Except for a pub and a ruined
D–Day fortress. In the patio bar
I meet my friend, among the floating seeds
Wafting in the wind off the feathery weeds.
I ask him about his family, the children's cries
Float above the tall weeds like the flying seeds;
During the winter he tells me they all survive
On income supplement, but as he has so many children,
That mounts up.

In the spring and through the summer they move here
And like nomadic Jews live among the waste places,
The embattled walks burst open by sieging grasses
Where they camp, not easy to pick out
With white tents in the feathery fields; they are Jewish.

We sit in the bar but do not drink more
Than one round, as we leave
The butterflies start to arrive in their thousands
From black chrysalids hidden in the concrete cellars
Of the ruined fortress, in their clouds
They are like peonies burst apart in fat petals,
Powder blue. One of the boys
Collects masses for lamp-fuel
By sweeping them out of the air
With his shirt, their fat
Gives a hot blue ghostly twilight flame. A younger boy
Unscrews a plastic bottle and refills my glass

With a yellow drink; he tells me
It is pollen-and-water shaken into his shirt
Before the caterpillars feast, the green worms
Of the blue butterflies. I lift up
The sherry-glass with the yellow life-substance in it
Of rooted plant and cursive butterfly
And swallow it in the bar of other fluids
Which have been fermented towards death
To get their spirit by bruising; and this pollen
Sweetened with nectar is the taste of the place
Of soil, castle, clear space and feathery seed,
Nectar-pumping butterfly and all else besides
On the height above the town where people can live for
 nothing.

LAST HOPE

The river sighs over the silken mudflats.
Sleeping, he resembles a casualty already.

He isn't so much of a pistol.
She draws the curtains heavy as sandbags.

A winking air-liner traverses the heavens.
The jowls of her cunt purr with snores.

Her tampons are her little swaddled
Christs, her bleeding opiums, her only hope.

FALMOUTH CLOUDS

I

The weather, opening and closing
Doors in the head,

Opening them gently like
A gradual suffusion of sun, or
Slamming thunder-splattered doors shut,

II

With a jangle of chairs disclosing
A writhing chain-locker of cloud
Slithering away into itself.

III

A chalky bust of Beethoven breaks open
On rows of ruffled theatre-chocolates which gleam
In the lightning; then, the stars
Walking in long chiffons of rain

IV

Where later chiffons are unrolled
Along a blue counter, a bolt of silk thumped down
So it unrolls with an astonishing perfume
And a blaze of white.

V

In the high wind implosions of dark-cloaked cloud
As through the stage trapdoors called 'vampires', plunge.

VI

An exploding herb-garden or laboratory
Shoots across the sky,
Arrests one's head and simultaneously
Across the inside of that dome
Plants horticultures of changeable perfumes.

VII

That ice-cathedral which built itself from nothing
But faith, is being shot from a cannon
For charity, with silver candlesticks and sonorous arches
And clergy scattering in their whitest surplices;

VIII

The cathedral was full of dazzling tablecloths
Which come rolling everywhere above on which are thrown
Dark shadows from much higher, of personages who appear
To be eating supper at a long table in an upper room.

IX

These clouds are packed with white gulls, while those
Are an aviary of dark rainbirds; when they collide
There is suddenly nothing but sun, hey presto.

X

Skywalkers with immense tension of presence
And extreme visibility and invisibility as well,
The cascades roll past, turn dragonish and then
They are all simple lace very high

On a blue robe which darkens with emergency generating
    stations
Black as floating mines of coal.

XI

I wake from a dream of crowned and grimacing white faces
To my bedroom window which crowds with vast white faces
    grimacing.

THE SNAIL'S PACE

The snail which carries its tower on its back
Quotes dew travelling the garden of salads
As the liner glides through its green waves

Snaffling the crisp spindrift, and with
Solemn undulations counterfeiting eternity.
The blood of slain men is the raven's drink,

Failing this tipple snails suffice.
Amazonian bird-priestesses rule the gates of death,
Tutela, the Goddess of the City, her emblem

Is the mural crown, signifying that everything
Within the walls is held in her thought
As the crown clasps her skull in a snail-grip.

The dark terrifies me because in it
I am awake but sleeping still, and there is
A pressure the colour of ravens, and there are

No cities, only the image of a snail
Gliding through Amazonian forests, which are
The green gates of death, for, emptying

Its incomparable spiral, which is
A masterpiece, the meat blows away.
(The motion remains, the screw of a propeller,

And his orgasm remains, achieved
At a snail's pace, as though
Drinking thirstily in reverse;

Her conch accepts his meat, and suddenly
The whole wilderness spirals upwards
And the priestesses bow, well-satisfied.)

CANNON

The evening wind of a shady beach blows
Sharply across the muzzle of a shipwrecked cannon;
It has lain here decades, black in the sands,

Aimed at the stars, battle-spent.
The sand scours the iron all day,
And all night long, spinning round and round

The belly of the night-hued iron
As stars spin in the round black heaven
With their faint ringing constantly

Of prism chasing prism over sable iron.

SNIFFING TOM

One who goes to and fro in summer
Sniffing the saddles of girls' cycles:
A Sniffing Tom.

The same chap (I know him well)
Farts in the bath and bites the bubbles:
He doubles as a *Snorkist.*

To secure his rank, the prince
Catches in his mouth the rank breath
Of the dying king: this is the *Air Apparent.*

He is crowned soon enough
And married with Holy Rites, which should
More properly be called *Holy Ruts,*

For after copulation the rank dream comes,
And he that dreams also sweats, farts, snores
And erects and should *revere*

Le rêve, its reverie, for he has dreamed
A classy one, that he unlocked
The school shed among the daffodils

And it contained 100 girls' cycles,
So he sleeps to dream again, and sweats,
And he is juicy; that is, *sapient*;

By Jiminy, this is sooth! by the twins
Of the two worlds, soothe, sleep
And wake; *by Gemini!*

FOR THE UNFALLEN

The spider plots its echoes of underground fastnesses;
You may find your way to the centre by the map of this
    gossamer;
Just so the tide-compass is marked through the jellyfish,
For it is the way-patterned sea-nettle.

The nautilus raises its fleshy sails
Among the cloudy misdirections of salt water but none mistakes
Its voyage, for the very air
Is patterned.

The sallow tunnels of the mice
Are the tunnels of wildfire in the grasses' roots,
The electrical township where lightning scurries
Hunting like mouse-ancestor down to the bedrock
After its strike. The nettle's venom
Is unshed light.

In this mist are fathomless pathways.
In my dream-body I enter the earth.
Perfume enlarges space, builds boulevards in it;
I am surrounded by entrances.
Her excitement is like an apron of waterfall;
I pass through this Fall into earth scented with gongs.

THE TOWN ALTERS SO THE
GUIDES ARE USELESS

I

Roomy white houses, pokey cafes,
Seawaves crisping in, smelling
Of receding storms, the beds
Everywhere of craftsman flowers,
Britain in Bloom, by their rude openings
Showing their craft of perfume,

The craft of perfume and electricity
Which is the town's name,
Its roots deep in the mines.

II

An old mine collapsing at midnight
Drives down the street like a furrowing earthquake;

Like marsh-bubbles of midnight
Mines rise through the houses
As the houses fall;

The airing-cupboard opens on a gritty precipice,
Your shirts fall into the unlaundered blackness
Scented with arsenic and mouldy copperas.

III

Even the trees are falling into the mines,
The woods are falling into the little hills
Which have such great undergrounds;

23

Even the trees that cure
By the continual utterance
Of their name-sound along the winds
And their perfume on the wind,
Even such trees fall as the hills open;

Even the healing tree
Which drew arsenious oxide up
And broadcast it in homoeopathic amounts,
Even this now descends
To its great white mother-lode in the dark.

Instead of hills
We are left with domes and whistling crags,
Ragged declivities as full of holes
As iron cheeses, copper cheeses.

IV

With delicacy and respect, our lamps lit,
We enter a broad gallery root-roofed
Half a mile down; our leader holds up his hand:
'Hush,' he says, 'do you smell that?'

So we turn our carbide lamps off, can better
Hear the water, and we dare
The bend of the corridor to where
The descended forests are glowing with fruit, in their orchard-
    caverns,
In all the hues of copper, tin and iron; he enters,

Our leader tastes a bronze apple, pronounces it good.

THE SILVERY OLD GOLDSMITH

I entered my old friend's shop
Where fiery mud refines to precious ornament;
A long furrow scored the carpet, and erased.
He loved to breed snakes, anywhere he could.

'Will you show me some
Of your more enthusiastic pieces,
Please?' 'Of course, my friend.'

The first was a tree of spikes of silver
Set in ebony, say two feet high;
It was white lightning branching within
Jet thunder, done
As a midget's hat-stand: 'It is a model
To scale of a radio-echo engraving on the sky
For a split-second all of Chopin's
Funeral march in the one figure,'
He placed it carefully in the air-vent where it played
Its sombre march over and over like
An implicate tuning-fork.

He saw I didn't care for the piece, so brought out
A small round table in silver-gilt, laid
As for a Cornish cream tea, but all metal as if
Midas had deigned to finger it. 'Look!' he seized
A fold of the silvery tablecloth and with
A tiny thunder-clap pulled it free – the cups and saucers
And tiny golden scones and dish of cream like clotted gold
Stayed put. I smiled appreciatively, but this wasn't it,
I decided to explore, and on the windowsill

I found a wide-mouthed jar, a quarter-filled
With straw-coloured plasma, half-a-dozen
Severed heads of snakes floated there, one
Still sleepily flexing its jaws, as if
Newly-reaped; I could see
The coarse red meat at the severed ends; the velours
At the window heaved, and I stepped quickly backwards:

'No, my friend, not a window-snake,
But my new tortoise-line . . .' and there glided into view
A most magnificent living jewel,
A tortoise with an emerald-and-ruby-studded test
The withered snake-head protruding from its dewlaps
And a tiny golden crown fixed to the sloping brow.
It began to climb the wall with silver claws,
'Do you make them out of the snakes?' He nodded.
'Then please make me a cruet-pair, my salt,
My pepper shall travel slowly past my guests
Loaded in gold and silver howdahs at my feasts,' I brushed
A tear away, 'I can hardly tell you, old friend, how glad I am
That at long last you have learned so beautifully
To carapace the snake.'

THE BLOUSE

I

It was her intention by adding
Great mutton-sleeves to her blouse
To expand the body social

Which greeted us by leaning tits on her forearms
Folded on the top of the bar which became
Because of the seriousness of her posture

Intelligible and purposeful, like a library
Of poetry with wonderful lettered titles
And corks. Now these sleeves

Puff like summer clouds with cuffs
Seven-eighths up to the elbow, and dressed thus
She can be more motionless than before, slowly

Distilling a pleasant knowing smile
Our of her blouse, out of the high neck
Out of the fermentation contained therein,

The moth-soft saloon of her skin.

II

These clothes to her surprise worked
Better than alcohol, so she might give up
Her barmaid's job; she found

Her perceptions primed in them, poring over
This negligible beetle in the soap-dish, as it scratches
Over the snowy scented slopes, the black mirrors

Of its torso heave, there a whole
Magician's planetarium heaves, a whole
Astrological herb-garden where beetles dine

On stars and planets, on pollen-grains
In every ordered shape, like Kepler's
Solids brought to earth, frail rooms

Of perfume, light and colour in these flowers
Puffed full of perfume like her mutton-sleeves.
She is, as we all are, full of pollen,

And knows at last her destination. The pub
Shuts at half-past two, near Kew, and she visits,
Blouse in full sail, all the oriental trees

Under glass drawing themselves up
Towards the sun to their full height
Puffing their mandarin chests, and she

The great and wonderful mutton-sleeved bush
Moving among the scented Taoists, like a bloused
Missionary approaching to be honoured

By the Emperor, who will with incense and the beauty
Of his attendants and their curious names
And windy whisperings, catch and concubine her.

THE BUTTERFLY ESSAYS

I

Lunch at the Butterfly Farm
Near the Sawmill; clouds of butterflies feeding
On the streams of sap from slaughtered wood.

II

The butterflies in fluttering chapters overflowing
The clouds of fragrance from the Mill; they are
Numerous as the sawdust, which is delicious to them,

III

Like the smell
Of the freshly-bought book of a sleepy man;
All the wings fluttering in a kind of unison, as
A draught flutters a tree of painted paper.

IV

The tubular winged tongues
Unpeeling into the syrupy mess
Of a punky banana, crushed in a saucer with plums.

In a parrot-cage a tarantula
Has given birth to itself, has opened
A lid in its back and climbed out
Pulling each limb in turn from its crusty stocking.
It leaves its shape there for a free trophy,
A tarantula-souvenir like a horn snuff-box.

VI

Black Velvet butterflies like exploded fragments
Of a velvet dinner-suit blown into nothing
But bows, still quivering; they tremble in the hibiscus
Like made-up evening ties dropped into a dressy bosom.

VII

Others vein their wings,
Become indistinguishable from the leaves
Among which they invent their boudoirs and take their
    passion.

VIII

The drowsy hibiscus with its Jungian blooms;
People in their unbutterflylike clothes
Lurch like dinosaurs among these quick spirits.

IX

Butterflies of the Nazis, the window
Of the hanging shed set with butterfly tanks
Like a beautiful land hovering beyond the noose.

X

The sandstone wall covered with basking butterflies,
The criminal set against it; at the shot
They rise like a multiplex soul carrying him off,
They settle on the wall again, on his face and clothes,
They copulate everywhere as his body cools.

XI

The shot man's last breath gasps from him
In a roll of spit like a chrysalis.
The firing-squad recovers its breath
Like fluttering butterflies seeking to alight.

XII

The dead man's reputation flares
Like a butterfly caught in a lamp-chimney up-draught;
His executioner with a breakfast cigarette
Burns a hole in his obituary so in the paper
There is a black-edged nothing shaped like a butterfly.

XIII

The forest's flesh and blood
Trooping into the Sawmills,
The butterflies multiply on the carnage
Now there are more of them than there are leaves
Their flesh becomes heavy as cigars, as lambs,
Now a family of three can dine on a butterfly,

Their eggs grow huge and delicate
This chef is noted for his butterfly omelettes;

Their chrysalids like birds' nests
Are esteemed by the Chinese,
Whose chefs wear rainbow-coloured chimney-hats.

TWO POEMS OF CONVENIENCE

Men with frightened and resigned faces
Mopping the floor, I almost
Stepped in the bloody water

But that was disrespectful. Somebody
Had cut their throat in the great mirror
Of the Waterloo Gents again, or maybe

Five or six people standing in a line
With one great blade simultaneously stroked
Across the throats; there was enough blood

For Grand Opera Guignol in great
Cornucopias and partly clotted
Hangmen's nooses, like Maria

Callas' period arriving during *Trouvatore*.

II

I wanted to look at my nosebleed
But the only mirror in the branch line loo
Was fastened to the condom-machine,

The reproducer, the mirror, fronting
The rubber-refuser dispenser, and I didn't care
To patronise this combination,

I will wipe the last blood off blind.
I got to our front door and found
That morning's *Guardian* tucked inside

One of a pair of wellies left outside;
Now the day's news would smell of rubber;
Except that when I opened the front door I was almost

Knocked down by the smell of roses
Like a great red-haired dog bounding to greet me;
There were so many that she had to put

The majority in the bath, so the loo
Looked like a miracle of St Elizabeth of Hungary
Who when taking meat to the partisans

Was challenged 'What are those stains upon
Your apron,' and she replied 'Roses,'
And her lap was found to be filled with roses;

But my wife had no idea who sent them
Nor did we ever know whose generosity
Had transfigured our bungalow until such time as

The sheaves rotted and were put out like carcasses for the fire.

IN THE LAB WITH THE LADY DOCTOR

The Old Woman resembles a fairy-tale princess
Who has stayed too long in her tower unrescued,
She precedes me among the benches, she puts
Her protective goggles on, and in this mood
Resembles that gnome who captured me; I look closer:
It is that gnome. She comes in again
With a flock of young men in white flapping coats
To whom she is goosegirl. I insist that the chemicals
On this side of the bench are strictly mine, and this includes
The bottle of gold salts, and the retort distilling
An infusion of bull-semen. There will be a fight, it's plain,
One of the young Privatdocents has his white coat off
    already
Underneath which he is naked, and in mock compliment I
    reach out
And shake him firmly by the wedding-muscle, upon which
He hits me all over maybe sixty times
In five seconds with karate blows, one of which
Catches me near my Person but safely thuds
On pubic bone, and I declare 'This assault should not
Have helped your case, but nevertheless this does not mean
That certain experiments cannot be performed in joint
    names . . .'
At my resolve, a spattering of applause, and the Old Girl
Crosses over from her young squires in dazzling plumage
And asks to see the bruises, so I strip off my shirt.
The marks of striking hands patter across my chest
And already the dark bruises are rainbowing like pieces
Of peacock tail. The young chap who inflicted them

Stands by, sniffing my retort's nozzle; with a shyly winning smile
'Will you give me a drink of this?' he asks. I feel like a fruit
Which has been bruised in order to ferment
Some delicious rare liquor; I say so; they applaud again.

FOUR POEMS OF LOVE AND TRANSITION

I

Her great thoroughfare,
Her sunlit valley; from the testes

Pass multitudes of liquid pearl. Her clitoris
Is a pearl stud on the jade step whereby

The jade pavilion is set on fire.
Thus the train was laid,

The rising stair, tides, docks, sluices,
Saltworks; now they drink

At the fountain of jade and raise
Their heads, dripping, and look around

At the chambers of paradise richly furnished
With the perfume which are prayers

Said on the prayer-mats of flesh and bone.

II

The greygreen clouds like giant jellyfish
Trailing their stings through the air.

I see a tendril wrap itself
Round the head of a woman;

She begins to shout at her child.
As the electrical air-works glide overhead

The beds of ore stretch open their blooms underground
Reflecting in petals of mirror their invisible light;

Upper weather a factory of fluorescences
Driving its lorries out over the sky

With their blackheadlights shining up our world
Like a blind man's fireworks;

I think fireworks were invented by prophets
To depict the workings of sferics everywhere:

Everything glitters. The brief shower
Is a foretaste of heaven. The huge

Vaulted chambers of wet light
Travel silently.

III

And a tentacle of that cloudy polypus
Slides down her arm like an ample sleeve,

Writes her words out of towering sources;
The travelling sky-springs and fountains

And the excavating rivers of the sky are telling
Of their millennial sources, their appointing tides

Joined and broken as they pass deep in the earth –
It is thunder heard in its sleeping form,

A rounded, black sound; its early result –
Apples.

The cat returning after his night's foray,
All the smells of it about him,
All the dews soaked deep into his midnight fur

By passage through the midnight grass
Which is the multitude observatory of the sky,
Each blade a green telescope poring upwards

A tube of green ichor-lenses
To which the whole earth puts her eye;
This observatory absorbs within itself

The rays of moon and stars, they sweat
Green recording-dew, these vessels,
A liquor which contains their transits,

And these cassettes of crystal are transferred
Like unction to the cat's black coat.
He is a walking astronomy.

He is liquor-of-moon in its animal form,
He is one whole-body deep-perfumed black moustache
Wandering thunderstruck full of kisses

Of astrological perfume through the grass verges.

LIKE A WALKING STICK

A kind of walking-stick with a black box
Strapped to it was my device for finding
When we had had enough, it gathered rage
From everyone around and discharged it in the form
Of a bolt of lightning. One day it picked out
All the circumcised people in the street
And stabbed its lightning near them into the ground
And made them dance; they were outraged, and this
Re-fuelled my box; I never learnt how to turn it
Completely off. It was deadly in the plane, there were

Those ice-cold stewardesses with their suits
And blouses open at the throats like memorialised
Abstract vaginas, and the plastic food they served
In invented solicitation, so the box grew hot
And punched a hole in the fuselage like tinfoil
And all of us sat still and screaming, pushing
Our backs into our chairs away from impact
Rigid in comfortable armchairs as the air screamed round us
Like a cinema audience watching its own death.
Fright drained the box; somehow there was
A skilful and sufficient landing, but those around me
Would not move, and it was as if I were
Completely alone and each of them had turned their lamp off.
I tried to wake a stewardess to her duty
But she sat on, chin tipped into cleavage. I got out
Of the plane, would I have to eat their flesh?
I pulled at the grey moss which quilted the fuselage,
It slid off in one place, whispering 'Am I

Edible?' At that moment all the trees and vines
And the animals in the vines began to whisper

Again, and the perfumes of the jungle twined
And the people in the plane got up and brushed
Themselves down and started gathering their baggage,
The Vee-necked stewardesses bobbing like winged heads
In the gloom. The grey moss
Was a sleepy lycopodium, condensed out of the extreme
    energy
Of the electric flash, like a shadow cast for an instant
By a photographer's bulb solidifying over the plane.
Some of the people were busy putting up tables
Inside the cabin and dressing in black and white clothes;
They were turning it into a hotel, a hotel
Beached in a jungle, and why not –
There was water, shelter, and personnel, now
All we needed was advertising; I looked for my
Black stick with the energy box strapped to it to help.

THE GREY GHOST

I had put out the whisky bottle like a cage of lions,
Tawny-maned and with a ferocious bite,
And the champagne, mild-mannered, feudally potent,
Chilled in its foil and every bubble intact,
But the ghost that came to me could not drink.

It had a heart to break, from the grey scraped face –
If only he would partake of our bottle of lions,
Or kiss the cool hand of our champagne,
Its dower-city of bubbling windows. I offered
An Asp, the cocktail called
Cleopatra's Cooler – it seemed
He would enjoy its venomous joke, but
He couldn't drink that either, or anything.

Did he come to counsel me, that ghost-friend job?
One young fellow I know has a whitebeard lodged
Nearer to him than anybody, perched
Within the waxy portal of his ear, who whispers
Behind his withered hand deep into his right brain; another
Consults with a black child invisible in the dark
Whose body is studded with attentive stars; another's
Silent invisible lover comes to her bed,
Communicates with fast hands running
Up and down her spinal keyboard in chills
That appear to blow off the estuary water. But what does
The grey scraped face come for, then, who cannot drink,

Who turns down all offers but the name of Void.

BUVEUR'S FAREWELL

Afore Ye Go!

I

Fellowsmokers,
It is a place of regulated sacrifice
Opening and closing at the proper times,
It is a house of spirits, and the quick
Fermentations of bruised barley, hops,
Resurrecting in our mouth, for
The beer talks; a place to incubate
The dream-pictures on the labels –
The titles and the names of spirits
Pictured with their habitations:
Schloss Buveur, Hexenbeers.

II

The brown light of God all around,
The mature autumnal light, soaked
Into the eyepods of pure ambrosia,
He says, leaning back, his elbow
On the bar, and sucks his cigarette,
An impalpable meal that will not stick
On a fork, a satisfactory intangible meal
Of talk in syllables of tobacco ash,
A communion in a temple of fellowdrinkers
Sharing the one round belly, one acrid breath.

III

Like Gods, we relish
The burnt sacrifice,
A meal of grey ghost
Inhaled, and we scatter
The yellow ashes
Of earth-brown beer used up
Pissed out clean,

For we are plumbers and purifiers
In the place where women
May not enter and which is dirtier
Than they would believe; we gaze
At the ceiling like astronomers
As we grab our pub-tackle
In dreamy relaxation,
Tributary stream, contributing,
Sings Piss-on-Boots.

IV

What are those glyphs
Of elemental names in gold-leaf
Hanging over the wide harbour view
Like spiritual airships plying
In mirror-writing?
Wines, Beers, Real Ale, Spirits,
And ourselves, crowding the deep mirrors
To capacity.

V

The benefits receding
Cigarettes and beer
Make small turds;

44

And the poet caught on a shingle
Seething with fag-ends

And dead men, which is what
With prophetic insight
They call empty bottles;

The dead men outnumber all the stars.

VI

The poet satisfying
The god of death in him;
He has his drunk girl friend along,
The direct opposite of his married wife,
Learned in the mysteries of the spirit
Driven out of the bruised flesh
Of John Barleycorn; in her presence
Holier than thou
Because drunker than thou, she
Deathlier in her sickness
Of drink than thou,
Stories taller than thou
More defecating than thou;
See where he stands, his two ends eloquent.

VII

And in the abrasive return
To the house of children and regular meals
Do these spirits satisfy actually?
It may be not, but it is still the way
To achieve the serenity of the woman
In her temple with her child
Where the raw is cooked and spooned

Into the hungry mouths sweet as flowers;
Accordingly we like hunters quaff the raw
Blood of the world out of barrels, the darting
Lightning of brandies. I say it is a womb-state,
A gentleman's lodge on the way home, and communion,
This meal taken in a male Sabbath
Or sewer, as you prefer.

VIII

Not just a meal
But a frenzy,
A three-and-a-half-hour's feast
With messages from Booze County;
The poet will get an idea, with trembling hand
Unhasp the small pocket pad or tablet . . .
The morning after – what disgrace!
The script too shaking to be read:
It is in Doctor Death's handwriting
Illegibly prescribing from his own pharmacy.

IX

Buveur
A gallon-an-hour man,
He is a river below the waist
Sliding towards the sea
He has drunk up his legs
Staggering from this church
Its stained glass
The quaffable brown light of God
Of the Real (meaning Royal) Ale Hall;

The depth and sheer well
Of opening time not deep enough
Not if it were all the beer in the world –
Why, he could leak it!

Or the globe of the world turned to beer
Whirling about the sun
In one great tun,
The cloud-capped towers of alcohol . . .

X

The skin tight at extreme
He has the notably bad idea of taking drink back
For the wife and the daughter –
In the brown earth-light
Of the spirit of earth
Passing through him,
At last he has the Sight!
The town is a harmony, the people orient wheat,
Each man is a spirit, the ships
In the harbour are one ship
Containing the same spirit
Who is three hundred men
All piss-pals.

XI

The beer is exactly that sweet
Mother-colour of iodine
Burning on that cut
Like whisky applied to the gullet,
Or, its cork-tip iodine-stained,
The cigarette's temporary fire.

XII

The liturgy is out of hand,
The brown eyes of God shining
From all the tables

47

We sit round tables
Furnished with pint-eyes,
Brown eyes in glass sockets –
We blind them all, one after another,
To obtain the Sight.

XIII

The dust interests,
And the ashes,
The goblet of dog-ends,
The sheer well of all beer

Interests

The brown light
Which is all places on earth at once
And the Mass of ships on the estuary
Interest, every detail seen
Through a precise microscope of pints and at once
Forgotten, because of the greater interest
Of the next grain of dust,
Or sufflation of the breeze, forgotten.
I am a wax face through which beer pours
Into a self greater than I can understand
Or remember, I feel eternal and young,
For I drink up the brown child of beer,
All beers are young beers,
I drink up the adolescent,
I drink up my childhood,
My health, my wealth, my safety.

XIV

Like a fruitcake this bar,
Like a ship this brown pub,

Like a galleon with its brown planking,
Its canvas of windows hissing,
It is pulling out over the beer-ocean;
This galley is afloat
Rowed by its beer-engines,
Manned by its slaves;

Piss-parliament is open
And I spit on the deck for luck.

XV

To stroll home from his church
After purification by pickling,
The brown light of God about him,
The khaki earth-light, the cackie air,
The women in their skirts of fine foam
And light ale in bottles of pubic hair,
All clothes drinking-clothes
The company of saints swaggering and staggering
From home to pub to home to pub
Pace down the bottomless well
To the brown basis of things.

XVI

The women shine, it is something
They distil from the booze
And redistil as they talk
Filling up the retort sip by sip;
The brown leather benches shine
With the polishing transit of
Boozers past, present and finished,
Things shine of themselves

At the bottom of this well, it is
Neo-platonic and like the brown back of books,
Study-pub, the volumes bound in glass
And with a handle and all precisely
The same length, or a prescribed length
Like easy books, and you can tell
In this library who is well-read by their gait.

XVII

Taking new surroundings
With each pint,
The feet carrying me without my volition
Back to the drowning-place
Where I sit under flavoured brown water
Drinking from never-empty glasses;
The whole air is my tears and urine;
We converse as the fishes do
By gobbling and presentiment,
The entire room is our bubbling voice
We are a school of people who drink
Like fish and are pissed as newts
And piss the brown of exhausted blood,
The mud of nicotine and decay,
Brown years, brown bread, mud bed,
Brown moss; the curtains
Sweep open, they have let
Too much light into this place, the drowned
Corpses puff up to the ceiling.

XVIII

Bed to pub to bed to pub
Despite wife and daughter –
They will take you on again,

Like ships, under their white sails
Blinding as blossom, masts of cherry-tree,
Who, blown along by their blossom,
Sail in willing to take you
Aboard again
Brown sailor
Bronzed by his voyages
Through his sabbaths and sewers
As ballast
Brown as the hills
Resolute to stay at home
Give it up, or maybe sup
On a few cans, or maybe
Out for a quick one
With that press-gang.

XIX

The moon smiles;
She knew it would not last;
There is drinking money where that came from;
She shines with her white meed
As though she were covered
With cherry-blossom, and, he swears,
A fragrance from the full arena
As it glides from behind the hills
And this clear sensation will surely last,
This cannot fade, he must catch it
In his glass, like the coin of a pint
Lying at the bottom of the pint
And he drinks the moon up, where
Is the next moon coming from;
The woman reaches into her lap,
Into her handbag; she will forgive
And she will buy him a last drink,

Even now, after all that, so he can
Catch his feeling and tell her about it,
And she will tell him back again so he can believe it,
And drink no more, in the small garden
At opening time among the blossom, watch
The moon blossom with her and in to bed;
Even now
With further silver coins
With further wells of tears
Reaches into her bag
For further wells of tears.

XX

All our sailing songs, our stamping
On deck-planking under sail
Of glass with reverse lettering,
Our voyages in the mirrors
Sounding to the well's note
Which fills the glasses not shatters them
With brown sweat of tuns, we live riotously
In this well until we are liverish bones
Wheeled in at opening-time, covered
With brown-spotted liver-moss and
There are always men off the rigs delighted to pay,
The beers flow through our fingers
Covered with Scandinavian calls
And German labels sounding like moss
And green halls and flowing dwarves' gold,
Pungent with their foreign colognes
Which in an international spirit
We absorb right into our bones
And deepest tubes, while

In her belly, a quart
Of pure water lies, containing a drinker;
Persuade her in pure fellowship
To have another mother's ruin and make her baby
So drunk he will sing all the way home.

XXI

The splatches of foam . . .
No, I am a liar; the book
Is not empty when it is drunk up;
I have the *Sighaagin* in sight, the veritable runes,
That secret script which announces everything;
This glass is not empty, it is foam-written upon;
I will take it home and decipher it further.
No, says my friend, you must drink up the letters;
I will, I say, and bind me up a new book, for I now know what
    they say,
Left in the glass, they read THE END,
Which I utterly deny; wash it away
Like a good fellow; wash it away with more.

XXII

Renew my book for me;
I raise it to my lips, blind book,
I close my eyes to drink,
I drink up all the runes
And they foam in my mind
Which is in my belly
After such long schooling
I have a runic belly
Listen to its chanting;
Make sense of that if you can.

XXIII

Time please, she chants
Breaking open the bubble room
Like a piggish litter,
Tumbling them out
Into the too-bright street
Snatching them from their rows of teats
For the sun to devour.

XXIV

For he has attended the sinister BROWN MASS,
The secret Mass of St Stagger;
He counts his steps home like time allowed,
Like mortal days remaining;
He must wait them out in his kindly bed
Where his ears fill with beer-sweat;
He tosses his head
Like a drinker throwing away pints;
I turn and turn again
Emptying those shells
That stain my pillows
With their murmuring waters;

I have drunk my inheritance;
That which disclosed grace to me
Closed it almost immediately.

XXV

Later, and maybe for ever,
I lift my glass,
And salute my fate;

My Grail
Which shows me everything at once;

I write of this as I drink
And find in the morning only spidertracks:
A few winged ideas caught,
And drunk up.

XXVI

Pallid animal, resembling lemmings,
Or the long-drowned from the sea inside,
Myself enclosing the womb-liquor I swim in,
Hauling myself on feeblest limbs
Out of a headache of my whole body,

I have stolen my head from myself,
I have stolen my hands, my legs, my liver,
Being stolen they are no good to me,
My hands cut off, my feet cut off,
My mouth sealed, my bride eloped.

Secret brown roots
Tap my night water, I sleep
Like the tuns in the cellar, fermenting.
Is this bed or bar-cellar?
Time is called again. I walk back
From the pub like blind Oedipus
Sockets weeping brown ale,
I will return again to these bars
In the town called Colonus, again and again
Until I can no longer be found;

Do you call these sanctuaries gracious
When they show me as I am to my lover and child first
And to myself only at the very last.